Limit of Liability/Disclaimer of Warranty

D1607351

Exams this study guide will help prepare you for

☐ ServSafe Food Protection Manager
☐ National Registry of Food Safety Professionals (NRFSP) International Certified Food Safety Manager (ICFSM)
☐ Prometric Certified Professional Food Manager (CPFM)

Recommended Study Tools

Download Gold Star Test Prep's Servsafe and CPFM Test Prep Android or iPhone app to gain access to hundreds of flashcards and take unlimited practice tests.

Principles of Food Safety

Foodborne Illness, Infection, and Intoxication

Every year, millions of people get sick from foodborne illnesses. A foodborne illness is any illness caused by eating foods or beverages that contain any biological, chemical, or physical contaminant. A foodborne illness is considered an outbreak when two or more people get the same illness after eating the same food. Food establishments can be held legally liable when someone gets a foodborne illness.

Foodborne infections are caused by eating food that contains living pathogens. Pathogens are disease causing microorganisms. In foodborne infections, symptoms have a delayed onset (symptoms don't appear right away).

Foodborne intoxication symptoms have a rapid onset. Foodborne intoxication is the result of eating food containing toxins. Toxins are produced by bacteria and cannot be killed by heat. Foodborne intoxication can also result from chemical contamination.

Children, the elderly, pregnant women, and those with weakened immune systems (cancer, HIV, etc.) are the most likely to get very sick from foodborne illnesses and are considered high risk populations.

4 Major Risk Factors

The 4 major risk factors that can lead to foodborne illnesses are: time/temperature abuse, improper personal hygiene, cross-contamination, and improper cleaning/sanitation.

Time/Temperature Abuse

Time and/or temperature abuse occurs when food is not cooked, thawed, or kept at the right temperature for the right amount of time.

Improper Hygiene

Examples of improper hygiene include, but are not limited to, not washing hands or wearing gloves while handling ready-to-eat (RTE) food, not washing hands after using the restroom, coughing and sneezing on food, and working while sick.

Cross Contamination

Cross contamination occurs when pathogens are transferred from one object to another. Examples of cross contamination include, but are not limited to, storing raw meat above RTE food, touching contaminated or raw meat and then touching RTE food, wiping food-contact surfaces with contaminated or dirty towels, etc.

Improper Cleaning and/or Sanitation

Pathogens can be transferred from one surface to another if proper cleaning and sanitation procedures are not followed. Examples of improper cleaning and/or sanitation include, but are not limited to, using the wrong sanitizing solution concentration; not storing wipe cloths in a sanitizer solution between uses; equipments and utensils not being washed, rinsed, and sanitized between uses; etc.

Major 8 Food Allergens

Most allergies are caused by milk, eggs, fish, shellfish, nuts, peanuts, wheat, or soy. Symptoms of allergic reactions can appear within a few minutes to hours after ingestion of the allergen. Symptoms can range from mild to severe and may include, but are not limited to, hives, itchy sensation, swelling, and respiratory distress. Anaphylaxis is a severe allergic reaction where the person's airway can become constricted; anaphylaxis can lead to death. Call the emergency department if a customer is experiencing a severe allergic reaction.

There should be a written policy on how to deal with allergies at the food establishment. There must be at least one person available per shift to answer questions about menu items and their allergen content.

When a customer indicates that they have an allergy, this must be written on the order. When preparing food for customers with allergies, ensure no ingredients contain the allergen, prep food in an area separate from all other foods and on cleaned/sanitized equipment, wash/dry hands and wear non-latex gloves. Do NOT place food prepared for customers with allergies on a tray with any other food, as cross contamination can occur. Cross contamination can also occur when frying food using oil that was used to fry something else (e.g. frying chicken in oil that was used to fry shrimp).

Time and Temperature Control for Safety (TCS) Food

Ready-to-eat and TCS food are more likely to cause illness. TCS food need proper time and temperature control to prevent pathogen growth. TCS food can also be referred to as Potentially Hazardous Food (PHF). Examples of TCS food include heat treated plant foods (cooked vegetables/fruits such as baked potatoes, baked beans), cut melons, sliced tomatoes, raw sprouts (alfalfa, bean, radish), tofu, soy burgers, cut leafy greens, garlic in oil, milk and dairy products, meat, shell eggs (except those treated to eliminate nontyphoidal Salmonella), poultry, fish, shellfish, and crustaceans.

Ready-to-eat food (RTE) is food that can be eaten without further preparation. Examples of RTE food include, but are limited to, cooked food, washed fruits/vegetables, deli meat, bakery items, sugar, spices, and seasonings, etc.

Use the acronym FAT TOM to help identify potentially hazardous food.
- ☐   F - food high in protein (meat, dairy, shellfish, eggs, etc)
- ☐   A - acidic (bacteria grows best in slightly acidic to neutral food; most TCS food have pH levels between 4.6 and 7.5)
- ☐   T - temperature danger zone (when food temperature is between 41F to 135F)
- ☐   T - time (maximum time PHF can stay in the temperature danger zone is 4 hours)
- ☐   O - some bacteria need oxygen (aerobic bacteria) to grow, some do not (anaerobic bacteria)
- ☐   M - bacteria need moisture to grow (you can make TCS food no longer hazardous by removing moisture; this is why bacon that is cooked to a crisp/dry is no longer potentially hazardous and can be stored at room temp.)

You can help keep food safe by controlling FAT TOM conditions.

Active Managerial Control/Person In Charge (PIC)

A food safety management system is a set of standard operating procedures (SOP) used to prevent foodborne illness. Active managerial control involves planning ahead for risks. The PIC is the person at a food establishment that manages operations and is authorized to take action to ensure food safety. The PIC must be able to demonstrate knowledge of food safety.

A key element in food safety is training all managers and employees. Employees only need to be trained in food safety as it relates to their assigned duties.

3 Types of Food Contaminants

There are 3 types of food contaminants: biological, chemical, and physical.

Biological Contaminants

Biological contaminants are the most significant source of foodborne illnesses. Biological contamination is caused by microorganisms. Microorganisms can be harmless or harmful. Disease or illness causing microorganisms are referred to as pathogens. There are 4 types of pathogens that can cause foodborne illnesses: bacteria, viruses, parasites, and fungi (which includes molds and yeast).

The FDA has called out six pathogens, called the Big Six, for being highly contagious and likely to cause severe illness. The Big Six pathogens are: Shigella spp., Salmonella Typhi, Nontyphoidal Salmonella (NTS), Shiga toxin-producing Escherichia coli (STEC) which is also known as E. coli, Hepatitis A, and Norovirus.

Bacteria

Bacteria doubles every 20 minutes and needs food to be slightly acidic to neutral (pH between 4.6 to 7.5) to grow. Adding very acidic food (below pH of 4.6) like vinegar, lemon, mayonnaise, etc. can help prevent some bacterial growth. Thorough cooking will kill bacteria, but freezing will NOT; bacteria will begin to grow once it's no longer frozen. The best way to prevent bacteria from causing a foodborne illness is through time and temperature control.

Bacteria	Source	Food Bacteria is Found In	Prevention
Salmonella Typhi	Lives only in humans and is found in the bloodstream and intestinal tract of people with typhoid fever.	Ready-to-eat foods and beverages	Wash hands, cook food to minimal internal temperatures
Nontyphoidal Salmonella	Farm animals	Poultry, eggs, meat, milk, dairy, tomatoes, peppers, cantaloupes	Wash hands, cook food to minimal internal temperatures
Shigella spp.	Human feces, flies	Food that is easily contaminated by hands (salads, produce, etc.)	Wash hands, cook food to minimal internal temperatures, control

			flies
E. Coli	Cattle intestines, infected humans	Raw and undercooked ground beef, produce	Wash hands and produce, cook food to minimal internal temperatures
Listeria	Soil, cattle, poultry	Deli meats, hot dogs, unpasteurized milk and dairy products, refrigerated smoked seafood	Wash hands and produce, cook food to minimal internal temperatures, do not eat raw dairy products, high risk populations should heat hot dogs and deli meats before eating
Clostridium botulism (produces lethal toxin)	Spores found in dirt and water	Incorrectly canned food, temperature-abused vegetables and baked potatoes, untreated garlic and oil mixtures	Control time and temperature, inspect canned food
Staphylococcus	Hair, skin, nose, and throat of infected humans	Any food that requires human handling	Practice proper hygiene

Viruses

Viruses are highly contagious and cannot be killed through normal cooking temperatures and cannot be killed through freezing. Viruses require a "host" (animal or human) to grow or multiply but can survive outside of a host for weeks on contaminated surfaces (door handles, utensils, etc.). Viruses cannot grow in food, they can be transferred through food. Foodborne illnesses caused by viruses usually occur through the fecal oral route.

The best way to prevent foodborne illnesses caused by viruses is to practice proper hygiene when handling food and food-contact surfaces.

Virus	Source	Food Virus is Found In	Prevention
Hepatitis A	Feces of those	Ready-to-eat food,	Wash hands, wear

	infected with Hepatitis A	shellfish from contaminated water	gloves when working with RTE food, purchase shellfish from reputable suppliers
Norovirus	Feces and bodily fluids of those infected with Norovirus	Ready-to-eat food, shellfish from contaminated water	Wash hands, wear gloves when working with RTE food, purchase shellfish from reputable suppliers

Parasites

Parasites require a host to live and reproduce and can range from single cell organisms to worms visible to the naked eye. Parasites are transferred from host to host by eating anything that has touched the stool of an infected person or animal. Parasites cannot be killed through cooking or freezing. Examples of parasites include:

- Trichinella - found in pork and wild game, can't be spread from human to human
- Anisakis - found in fish/seafood and causes a tickling sensation in the throat
- Giardia - found in contaminated water and causes diarrhea and abdominal cramps

The best way to prevent foodborne illnesses caused by parasites is to purchase food from reputable suppliers and making sure that fish that will be served raw or undercooked have been properly frozen by the supplier.

Biological Toxins

Biological toxins can be found in certain fish, shellfish, plants, and mushrooms; they can also be produced by bacteria (as is the case with botulism). Toxins, such as histamines, can be produced by fish pathogens when proper time and temperature controls are not followed and cause Scombroid poisoning; this can occur with tuna, bonito, mackerel, and mahi mahi. Scombroid poisoning symptoms include, but are not limited to, swelling or rashes around the neck/chest, tingling/burning sensations around the mouth, itchy skin, vomiting, diarrhea, etc. Ciguatera toxin can be found in barracuda, snapper, grouper, and amberjack. Ciguatera fish poisoning can cause blurred vision, numbness around the mouth, vomiting/diarrhea, and paralysis. Shellfish can be contaminated when they eat algae that have toxin.

In general, people will experience symptoms within minutes of eating a toxin. Symptoms may vary and may include, but are not limited to, neurological symptoms such as tingling, unusual sensations, difficulty breathing, hives, etc.

Toxins cannot be destroyed through cooking or freezing. The best way to prevent toxin poisoning is to purchase food from reputable suppliers and follow proper time/temperature controls.

Fungi

Fungi are called spoilage organisms because they spoil food, but generally do not cause illness. Yeast is a fungi that spoils food and drinks, typically those that are high in sugar. Mold is a fungi that is green/grey in color; certain molds can be dangerous and produce toxin. Moldy food should be discarded.

Chemical Contaminants

Chemicals can contaminate food if they are not properly stored or used. Examples of common chemical contaminants include, but are not limited to, cleaners, sanitizers, pesticides, hand lotion, hair spray, etc. Toxic metals can leach into food if acidic food is stored in metal containers such as copper, brass, tin, galvanized cookware, pewter, painted pottery, etc. MSG, sulfites, and too much additives can also be considered chemical contaminants

Symptoms of chemical poisoning will vary depending on the chemical consumed and typically occur within minutes of ingestion. Call the Poison Control Center if chemical poisoning is suspected.

To prevent chemical contamination:
- Only use chemicals approved for use in a food service operation and follow the manufacturer provided directions and safety precautions.
- Use and store chemicals (lotion, hair spray, cleaners, etc) away from food, food prep areas, and food contact surfaces. Food and chemicals must be separated by space and partitions. NEVER store chemicals above food or food-contact surfaces.
- Cover food when using chemicals.
- Make sure the manufacturer's labels on chemical containers are readable.
- Have material safety data sheets (MSDS) for all chemicals. MSDS are important to have for first aid information.
- Do not add sulfites to food that is intended to be eaten in its raw form.

Physical Contaminants

A physical contaminant is anything that can be seen such as fish bones, dirt, jewelry, rodent droppings, etc. Physical contaminants can cause choking, cuts, dental damage, pain, etc.

To prevent physical contamination:

- Make sure employees do not wear jewelry in food prep areas, wear hair restraints, and practice proper hygiene.
- Inspect the food you receive and serve.
- Regularly inspect storage area for pests.
- Store and cover food properly.

Preventing Deliberate Contamination of Food

To help prevent deliberate contamination of food, use the FDA created food defense procedures based on the acronym ALERT.

- **A**ssure: Only purchase from approved and licensed vendors, supervise product deliveries and request that delivery vehicles are locked or sealed.
- **L**ook: Staff should be aware of surrounding and make notice of any suspicious activity. Limit access to food prep and storage areas. Store chemicals in a secure location.
- **E**mployees: Only permit access to authorized personnel. Identify all visitors and verify credentials. Do background checks on all employees.
- **R**eports: Any activity related to food defense should be documented: training docs, background checks, receiving logs, etc.
- **T**hreat: Identify what you will do if a threat is suspected. If any food is suspect, contact authorities immediately and make sure the food is kept and separated to assist the health department investigation. Maintain an emergency contact list.

Preventing Foodborne Illnesses

Cross Contamination Prevention Methods

To prevent cross contamination:
- Don't use the same knife to cut meat and then cut greens without cleaning or sanitizing the knife. Have designated cutting boards (one for meat, one for greens, etc.).
- Make sure all equipment/work surfaces/utensils are cleaned and sanitized before use or when changing tasks.
- Wash hands and change gloves between tasks.
- Don't store or prep raw foods near cooked or ready to eat foods.
- Don't store raw meat above cooked or RTE foods in the fridge.
- Buy food that does not require much preparing or handling.

Time/Temperature Abuse

The Temperature Danger Zone, 41F degrees to 135F degrees, is the temperature zone in which bacteria survives and grows. Cold food should be kept below 41F degrees and hot food should be kept above 135F. The maximum time TCS food can stay in the temperature danger zone is 4 hours, 6 hours if the food is kept under 70F degrees. The 4 hours includes the total time to receive and inspect the food package, time to prepare the food, etc. The 4-hour clock starts over once the food is brought to a temperature outside of the danger zone (e.g. refrozen, re-cooked). Sometimes food can be returned to a safe condition by reheating or refreezing if it has not been in the temperature danger zone for more than two hours; this process is called reconditioning. Food must be discarded after the time limit is reached.

Food handlers should be trained to know which food items should be checked, how often to check the food item, and what to do if the time or temperature standards are not met (e.g. refrozen, re-cooked, or throw away). They should also be recording the temperature of food items regularly. The temperature and time the temperature was taken should be written in a log and placed near coolers, freezers, prep areas, and next to cooking or food holding equipment.

The danger zone range may be different in your local jurisdiction, so check your local health department.

Monitoring and Measuring Temperatures

Temperatures must be monitored at all times (receiving, cooking, cooling, hot holding, etc.) to ensure they are outside the temperature danger zone.
- When measuring temperature, put the thermometer in thickest part of the meat, fish, or chicken.

- When measuring temperature for packaged foods, put the thermometer between 2 packets.
- When measuring temperature for milk, soup, or salad, open the container and check the internal temperature; make sure the thermometer does not touch the bottom or sides of the container.

Thermometers

Thermometers must be able to read from 0F to 220F degrees. Food thermometers must be accurate within 2F degrees. Thermometers used to measure air temperatures must be accurate within 3F degrees. Thermometers should be calibrated regularly to maintain their accuracy. Calibrate thermometers when they are new, dropped, used between extreme temperatures, before deliveries arrive, and before each shift. Some thermometers can only be calibrated by the manufacturer and some thermometers cannot be calibrated and must be replaced.

There are two methods to calibrate a thermometer: the "ice point method" or "boiling point method". The **"ice point method"** involves filling a container with ice and water, stirring the water for an even temperature, and putting the thermometer in the container for 30 seconds; it should read 32F. If the thermometer does not read 32F, adjust the thermometer until it reads 32F. The **"boiling point method"** involves putting a thermometer in boiling water; it should read 212F at sea-level, adjust otherwise. The "ice point method" is preferred because it is easier and safer and you don't have to think about the boiling point changing with altitude.

Do not use glass thermometers or thermometers containing mercury as they can shatter and contaminate food; they can only be used if they are enclosed in a shatterproof casing.

For records and documentation, internal temperatures measured using probe type thermometers are required.

Types of Thermometers

There are 3 types of commonly used thermometers: bimetallic stemmed, thermocouples and thermistors, and infrared lasers.

Bimetallic Stemmed Thermometers
Bimetallic stemmed thermometers can measure temperatures from 0F to 220F degrees. They can be used to measure food that have just been cooked, food in hot or cold holding, or when receiving food deliveries. They can NOT be placed in food while the food is being cooked.

To measure the temperature of food using a bimetallic stemmed thermometer, you need to insert the metal stem into the food up to the dimple (about 2-3 inches). The dimple on the stem marks the end of the temperature sensing area of the thermometer. Bimetallic stemmed thermometers are used to measure temperatures of thick foods, it should not be used to measure the temperature of thin foods like fish fillets. Bimetallic stemmed thermometers should be used to measure the temperatures of roasts, casseroles, soups, and protein salads such as chicken/tuna salad.

Thermocouples and Thermistors

Thermocouples and thermistors have a metal probe with the temperature sensing area on the tip of the probe; this allows them to be used to measure the temperature of both thick and thin foods because it does not need to be inserted as deep as bimetallic stemmed thermometers to get a good reading. They only need to be inserted about ¼ inch or deeper. Temperatures are displayed digitally.

Thermocouples and thermistors have various probe attachments. Immersion probes are used for measuring liquids such as soup or frying oil. Surface probes are used for checking the temperature of flat cooking equipment such as grills. Penetration probes are used for checking the internal temperature of food and are useful for checking the temperature of thin foods such as hamburger patties. Air probes are used to check the temperature of refrigerators and ovens.

Infrared (Laser) Thermometers
Infrared (Laser) thermometers only measure surface temperatures. They do not need to touch the surface of food or equipment to measure the temperature which is good because it helps prevent cross contamination. The downside is it cannot measure the internal temperatures of food and cannot measure air temperature.

When using infrared thermometers, hold the thermometer as close to the surface as possible, without actually touching the surface. There should be nothing between the thermometer and the surface of the food or equipment. Do not take readings through glass or metal, such as aluminum foil.

Food Preparation

Before preparing any food, make sure all workstations, cutting boards, equipments, and utensils are cleaned and sanitized. To prevent food from sitting out too long, only remove as much food as you can prep in a short time from the cooler and return it to the cooler quickly or cook it promptly.

If you are working with food or color additives:
- Only use additives allowed by regulatory authorities.
- Only use the amount of additives permitted by law.
- Never use additives to alter the appearance of food.
- Do NOT sell produce that was treated with sulfites before it was received by the food establishment.
- Never add sulfites to food that will be eaten raw.

Thawing Foods (4 ways)

Temperature abuse often happens during thawing and preparing food. Never thaw food at room temperature. There are 4 proper ways to thaw food.
- Thaw food in the refrigerator, maintaining a temperature of 41F or lower.
- Thaw food under cold and drinkable (potable) running water. The water temperature must be 70F or lower, food must be fully submerged, and the water must be continually flowing. Always use a clean and sanitized food prep sink.
- You can thaw food in a microwave if it will go immediately into the cooking process; microwaves can't be used to thaw products that will be cooked at a later time.
- Thaw food as part of cooking process, food goes from the freezer and immediately into being cooked.

If thawing frozen fish packaged in reduced-oxygen packaging (ROP), remove the fish from the package before thawing it under refrigeration. If thawing under running water, remove the fish from the package before or immediately after thawing it under running water.

Cooling Food

Cooked TCS must be cooled from 135F to 41F within 6 hours; it must be cooled from 135F to 70F within 2 hours and you then have the remaining hours to cool it from 70F to 41F. If the food is not cooled to 70F within 2 hours, it must be reheated and then cooled again. If food is not cooled within 6 hours, it must be discarded or reheated to 165F

When cooling food, do NOT cover it. To reduce cooling time: divide food into smaller portions, use shallow trays, stir food frequently, and use ice wands or ice water baths. Do NOT cool large amounts of hot food in a cooler.

Reheating Food

There is no temperature requirement when reheating food for immediate service.

If you are reheating food for hot holding, it must be reheated to a minimum internal temperature of 165F for at least 15 seconds, within 2 hours. Roasts, commercially processed or packaged food, and hermetically sealed food must be reheated to a minimum temperature of 135F within 2 hours. Once food reaches a temperature of 165F, it must be held at temperature of 135F or higher.

Preparing Produce

All fruits and vegetables must be washed and dried before they are cut and cooked. When washing lettuce or spinach, remove the outer leaves and pull all the leaves apart, so they can be washed thoroughly. Produce may also be washed in water containing ozone to help control pathogen growth.

When soaking or storing producing in standing water or ice-water, do NOT mix different produce or multiple batches of the same produce.

Sliced or cut produce or vegetables need to be held at temperatures of 41F or lower.

Do not serve raw sprouts to high risk populations, such as those in day care centers and nursing homes. If juice is not pasteurized, you need a warning label; you may not serve unpasteurized juice to high risk populations.

Salads that contain TCS foods should be discarded 7 days from when the original TCS food (e.g. chicken, tuna, etc.) was cooked or cooled, not the date the salad was assembled.

Eggs and Egg Mixtures

Check with your local regulatory authorities to see if pooled eggs are allowed. Pooled eggs are eggs that have been cracked and put into the same container. Pooled eggs need to be held at 41F or lower or cooked immediately.

If serving high risk populations, eggs and egg mixtures that will not be fully cooked, must be pasteurized. You may use unpasteurized eggs if it will be cooked fully.

Ice

Ice must be made from safe drinking water. Ice used for cooling food can't be used for direct consumption.

Ice scoops must be stored on clean and sanitized surfaces or stored in ice with the handle completely out of the ice.

Never use a glass or cup to scoop ice.

Cooking Requirements

Foods should be cooked to the correct minimum internal temperature. While cooking reduces pathogens in food, it does not destroy spores or toxin.

If you serve food with raw or undercooked eggs, raw fish, rare steak, etc., you need to provide a "consumer advisory". Never serve high risk populations raw or undercooked meat; meat cannot be "cooked to order" for high risk populations.

Food	Cooking Requirement
poultry (ground or whole); stuffing made with fish, meat, or poultry; stuffed meat, seafood, poultry, or pasta	cooked to a minimum internal temperature of 165F for at least 15 seconds
all ground meats except poultry; injected meat such as brined ham; mechanically tenderized meats; ratites such as ostrich or emu	cooked to a minimum internal temperature of 155F for at least 15 seconds
unpasteurized shell eggs that will be placed in hot holding	cooked to a minimum internal temperature of 155F for at least 15 seconds
all other meats not mentioned above; seafood; steaks, pork chops, beef, veal, lamb; commercially raised game	cooked to a minimum internal temperature of 145F for at least 15 seconds
unpasteurized shell eggs prepared for immediate service	cooked to a minimum internal temperature of 145F for at least 15 seconds
roasts of pork, beef, veal, or lamb	cooked to a minimum internal temperature of 145F for at least 4 minutes

fruits/vegetables/grains/rice pasta cooked for hot holding	cooked to a minimum internal temperature of 135F (no minimum time)

Cooking Food In A Microwave

When cooking food in a microwave:
1. Cover the food to prevent it from drying out.
2. Rotate or stir the food halfway through to heat the food more evenly.
3. Let the food stand for two minutes after heating to even out the heat.
4. Check the food temperature in at least two places. Meat, seafood, poultry, and eggs cooked in the microwave must be cooked to a minimum temperature of 165F.

Partial Cooking

Partial cooking or parcooking is the practice of partially cooking food during prep and then finishing cooking it right before service. Regulatory authorities will require you to submit documents describing partially cooked food will be prepped and stored; the documents must contain the following information:
- How requirements will be monitored and logged and what actions will be taken if the requirements are not met.
- How items will be marked after the initial cooking to indicate they need further cooking.
- How items will be separated from RTE food during storage after the initial cooking.

The steps for partially cooking meat, seafood, poultry, or eggs are below:
1. Do not cook the food for longer than 60 minutes during the initial cooking.
2. Cool the food immediately.
3. Freeze or refrigerate the food after cooling it. The food must be held at a temperature of 41F or lower.
4. Heat or cook the food to the required minimum internal temperature before serving.

Practices That Require a Variance

A variance is a document, issued by regulatory authorities, that allows you to deviate from a regulatory requirement. You will have to submit a HACCP plan, which documents how you will address food safety risks, when applying for the variance.

Food preparation practices that require a variance include:
- Smoking food or adding additives, such as vinegar, as method of preservation instead of flavoring.
- Curing food.
- Packaging unpasteurized fresh juices on-site for sale at a later date, unless you put a warning label that complies with local regulations.

- Packaging food using a reduced oxygen packaging method; this includes MAP, vacuum-packed, and sous vide food.
- Custom processing (butchering/handling) of animals for personal use and not for sale or service in the food establishment.
- Operating a shellfish tank used to store or display shellfish that are offered for human consumption.
- Serving raw or undercooked shellfish.
- Sprouting seeds or beans

Food Holding

Hot/Cold Food Holding

Hot food must be held at a temperature of 135F or higher. Cold food must be held at a temperature of 41F or lower. Measure the temperature every 4 hours. If hot food drops below 135F for more than 4 hours, it must be discarded; if less than 4 hours, it can be reheated. If cold food is held at a temperature of 41F or below, it may be held for 7 days.

If you are NOT primarily serving a high risk population, you may be able to hold food, without temperature control, for a short period of time.

You can hold cold food without temperature control for up to 6 hours if the following conditions are met:
- Hold the food at 41F or lower before removing it from refrigeration.
- Label the food with the time you removed it from refrigeration and the time it must be thrown away (6 hours from the time it was removed from refrigeration).
- Food must not exceed 70F; food that exceed 70F must be thrown out.
- Food must be served or thrown out within 6 hours.

You can hold hot food without temperature control for up to 4 hours if the following conditions are met:
- Hold the food at 135F or higher before removing it from temperature control.
- Label the food with the time you removed it from temperature control and the time it must be thrown away (4 hours from the time it was removed from temperature control).
- Food must be served or thrown out within 4 hours.

Serving Food

Kitchen Staff

Food handlers must wear single-use gloves when handling RTE food or use tongs, spatulas, etc. to handle food. Utensils should be cleaned and sanitized after each task; if utensils are being used continuously, they need to be cleaned and sanitized at least every 4 hours.

Serving utensils can be stored in the food as long as the handle stays above the rim of the container. Ice cream or mash potatoes scoops can be stored under running water or in a container of water kept at 135F or higher.

If local regulations allow, take-home boxes can be refilled if they were designed to be reused, provided to the guest by the food establishment, and cleaned and sanitized. Take-home beverage containers can be refilled if the beverage is not a TCS food, it is being refilled for the same guest, and the container can be cleaned at home. Rinse the container with hot water under pressure before refilling.

Service Staff

Never touch the food contact surfaces of dishes, utensils, drinking glasses, etc. Hold dishes from the bottom or edge of the dish. Carry glasses in a rack or tray; do not stack them. Hold individual glasses by the stem, middle, or bottom.

You may not re-serve food, except under the following conditions:
- The food is pre-packaged and unopened.
- Bottles of condiments (ketchup, mustard, etc.)

Self Service Areas/Buffets

Salad bars and buffets need to be protected with sneeze guards that are no higher than 14 inches above the counter and extend beyond the food by at least 7 inches. Food may also be stored in display cases or their own packaging for protection. Whole fruits and vegetables, nuts in shells, and anything that requires additional peeling or hulling before being eaten, do not need to be protected.

Only cups are reusable; customers must use clean plates each time. All food contact equipment and surfaces should be cleaned at least every 4 hours.

Off-Site Service

Before transporting, label the food containers with the use-by date and time, and reheating and service instructions. The food should be packed in insulated food-grade containers that prevent food from leaking or mixing. Remember to check the internal temperature of the transported food.

Vending Machines

Check vending machines daily for expired food. Fresh fruits with edible peels should be washed and wrapped, before being put into a vending machine.

Purchasing, Receiving, and Storing Food

Purchasing

Only purchase from approved suppliers and according to federal, state, local laws. You can ask to view a suppliers inspection report from the USDA, FDA, or third party inspector.

Receiving

When you receive a delivery, check the packages for color, odor, texture, pest activity, temperature, and spoilage. If you must reject an item, set the item asides and tell the delivery person. Log the incident on the invoice and be sure to get a signed adjustment or credit slip for the returned items. If deliveries occur after business hours, such as is the case with key drop deliveries, the delivery must be inspected once you arrive at work.

All TCS foods must be received and kept colder than 41F or hotter than 135F. In some jurisdictions, milk, shellfish, and eggs may be received at 45F or lower, but must be brought to 41F or lower within 4 hours. The internal temperature of shellfish when received must be less than 50F. Due to parasites, seafood intended to be consumed raw or partially cooked, must be frozen to -31F for at least 15 hours or -4F for at least 7 days by you or a seafood processor. Most non-frozen perishable food should be received alive or at temperature of 41F or 45F.

Packaging

Items should be delivered in their original packaging with the manufacturer's label. Reject items that are missing labels, have labels that are missing the expiration or use-by date, or have tears or dents. Reject cans that have signs of dents, holes, or leaks, or are swollen.

- Live shellfish must be alive and must arrive with the shellstock id tags attached to containers. Shellstock id tags tell you when and where the shellfish were harvested so you can determine if the shellfish were from an approved source. Tags must remain attached to containers until containers are empty. Once a container is empty, shellstock tags must be maintained for 90 days.
- Fish that will be eaten raw or partially cooked must be received with documents stating that the fish were correctly frozen. Farm raised fish must have documentation affirming that the fish were raised according to FDA standards. The documents must be kept for 90 days from the sale of the fish.
- Fish should be delivered and stored in crushed ice. The eyes should be clear and bulging; the flesh should be firm and elastic.
- Meat and poultry must have United States Dept of Agriculture (USDA) inspection stamps on the package.

- Reject meat, fish, or poultry that is slimy, sticky, dry, or has soft flesh that leaves an imprint when you touch it.
- Vacuum-packaged meats must be rejected if the packaging is bloated or leaking. The package can be purple upon arrival and turn red when exposed to air; this is called blooming.
- Frozen foods with signs of thawing (ice crystals, water puddles, etc.) should be rejected.
- Eggs need to be clean with shells intact. Liquid eggs and milk must be pasteurized and grade A.
- Products labeled UHT (ultra high temperature), such as liquid coffee creamer, do not need refrigeration until opened.

Storage

Any food not easily identifiable must be labelled. Food must also be labeled if they are not in their original containers. Labels should also contain a date mark. Food packaged in the establishment for customer use at home must include the following information in the label:
- Name of the food
- Quantity of food
- List of ingredients and sub-ingredients in descending order by weight.
- List of artificial colors and flavors in the food.
- Chemical preservatives.
- Name and address of the manufacturer, packer, and distributor.
- Major food allergens.

Ready to eat food must be date marked if they are held for longer than 24 hours. The label should indicate the sell-by, use-by, or expiration date. Ready to eat food can be stored for 7 days if kept at a temperature of 41F or lower; it must be thrown away after that date. The day the product was prepared is counted as day 1.

Other than waterproof containers or bottles, cans, or milk in plastic crates, all food and equipment must be at least 6 inches off floor and away from walls. Store food and equipment in clean and dry areas in their original food grade containers, away from lockers, sewer lines, etc. Room temperature should be between 50F-70F with humidity between 50% to 60%.

Food should be rotated first in, first out (FIFO); basically, use the oldest food first.

Cold Storage

Refrigerator temperatures must be 38F-39F, measured in the warmest part of the unit. Refrigerator thermometers must be accurate to within 3F. Do not overcrowd a refrigerator or use solid shelves, both can interfere with air flow and cooling. Do not store hot food in a refrigerator, it can raise the temperature of the fridge. Food can be stored in the fridge if it is less than 70F.

Store raw meat, poultry, and seafood away from RTE food. If they cannot be stored separately, store them according to how high the cooking temperatures needs to be (RTE at the top, seafood or whole fish, whole cuts of beef or pork, ground meat or ground fish, whole or ground chicken at the bottom).

Personal Hygiene

Personal Cleanliness

- Fingernails needs to be clean, short, and unpolished; no fake nails or extensions unless gloves are worn at all times. Nail polish should not be worn because it can hide dirt under nails.
- If hands or wrists have any open cuts or sores, employees must wear bandages and gloves or a finger cot.
- Employees should not smoke, eat, drink, chew tobacco or gum near food, equipment, food prep areas, or food service areas. If your local jurisdiction allows drinking, drinks must be stored in a cup with a lid and straw.
- Do not allow employees to come into work in their uniforms (their personal clothing may be contaminated). Employees should change into uniform at a designated workplace changing area. If there is no workplace changing area, an apron can be worn over their clothing.
- Change dirty uniforms or aprons as necessary to avoid contaminating other items. Aprons should be removed when leaving prep areas (e.g. remove aprons before taking out the garbage or using the restroom). Never wipe your hands on your apron.
- Hair must be restrained with a hat, hair net, or some device to prevent hair from falling. Employees with facial hair should wear a beard restraint.
- Avoid wearing jewelry, only one simple metal ring is allowed. Watches and medical bracelets are NOT allowed. Jewelry is not allowed because it can harbor bacteria, fall off and become a physical contaminant, and is a personal safety hazard to an employee if it gets caught in equipment.

Handwashing

Handwashing is the most important part of personal hygiene. Staff members must wash their hands in a sink designated for handwashing; they must NEVER wash their hands in sinks used for food prep, dishwashing, or sinks used for discarding waste water. Gloves and anti-bacterial gel are not substitutes for hand washing; never use an anti-bacterial gel in place of handwashing. Anti-bacterial gel may be used after handwashing; wait for the gel to try before touching any food or equipment.

If a food handler touches food or food contact surfaces with unclean hands, you must throw away the contaminated food and clean the contaminated equipment.

Food handlers must wash their hands:
- When they first arrive to work.
- Before preparing food or working with clean equipment.

- Before putting on single use gloves.
- After using the restroom.
- After touching their body or clothes.
- After eating, drinking, smoking, or chewing gum or tobacco.
- After handling dirty items.
- After handling raw meat, seafood, or poultry.
- After taking out the garbage.
- After touching any animals (alive or dead).
- After handling chemicals.
- After changing tasks (before beginning a new task).
- After leaving and returning to the kitchen or food prep area.
- After using electronic devices (cell phones, etc.)

Hand washing stations should be near food prep areas and must be in bathrooms, must have hot (100F or hotter, 120F in CA) and cold running water, soap (any kind), hand drying machine and/or towels, trash can for paper towels,and a sign saying "employees must wash hands" in all languages spoken by your employees.

To properly wash hands:
1. Wet hands and forearms with warm water. The water should be 100F or hotter, 120F or hotter in CA.
2. Apply soap and wash hands for 20 seconds (10-15 seconds of actual rubbing). Do not forget to clean under fingernails and between fingers.
3. Rinse with warm water and dry hands with disposable towels, a heated air hand drying device, or a room temp high velocity device.
4. Use a paper towel to turn off the faucet and open the door when leaving a restroom.

Gloves

Single-use gloves can only be used for one task and then must be discarded. Single-use gloves should always be worn when handling ready to eat food. The only exceptions are when washing produce or when handling ready to eat ingredients that will be further cooked.

Only single-use gloves can be worn when handling food. Never wash and reuse gloves. Never blow into gloves or roll gloves to make them easier to put on.

Single-use gloves should be changed:
- When gloves become dirty or torn.
- Before starting a new task.
- After handling raw meat and before handling ready to eat food.
- After 4 hours of continuous use.

To put on gloves:

1. Wash your hands before putting on gloves. You do not need to wash your hands every time you change gloves as long as you are performing the same task and your hands have not been contaminated
2. Avoid touching the gloves as much as possible; hold the gloves by the edge when putting them on.
3. Check for any tears on the gloves.

Cleaning and Sanitizing

Non-food contact surfaces only need to be cleaned and rinsed. Food contact surfaces must be cleaned, rinsed, and sanitized. Food contact surfaces must be cleaned and sanitized:
- After they are used.
- Before working with a different type of food or different type of raw fruit or vegetable.
- Any time a surface may have been contaminated.
- After 4 hours of continuous use.

Some equipment, such as soft-serve machines, must be cleaned and sanitized every day unless otherwise directed by the manufacturer.

Cleaning (4 types: detergents, degreasers, delimers, abrasives)

Cleaning is the process of removing all food debris or soil from any item or surface. All cleaners must be stable, non-corrosive, and safe to use.

Type of Cleaner	Purpose
detergent	removes dirt and food from surfaces; use with hot water; used for dishes and equipment washed in 3 bay sinks
degreasers	used to remove heavy grease
delimers	acidic; used to remove mineral buildup
abrasive cleaning agents	used for heavy baked-on or cooked-on food

Sanitizing (2 ways: heat or chemical)

Sanitation is the process of killing pathogenic microorganisms. All food contact surfaces must be sanitized after they are cleaned and rinsed. There are two methods to sanitize items: the heat method and the chemical method.

Heat Method

The heat method involves soaking items in plain hot water or running items through a high-temperature dishwasher.
- If soaking items in plain hot water, items must be submerged in hot water (at least 171F) for at least 30 seconds

- If running items through a dishwasher, the water must be between 180F and 194F.

Chemical Method

The most common types of sanitizers are chlorine, iodine, and quaternary ammonium ("quats"). Another type of sanitizer are detergent-sanitizer blends which are often used in places that have two compartment sinks; you first clean items with the detergent-sanitizer blend and then use the detergent-sanitizer blend a second time to sanitize it.

To use sanitizers effectively, you have to use the correct concentration, temperature, contact time, water hardness (the amount of minerals in the water), and pH. Sanitizer concentrations are listed in parts per million (ppm). Too much sanitizer can be toxic, but too little may be ineffective. Use test strips to test for the correct sanitizer concentrations; the temperature of the sanitizing solution must be below 120F or the test strip may give inaccurate results. Check the sanitizer concentration often because hard water, food particles, and leftover detergent can reduce the effectiveness of sanitizers.

Sanitizer	Required Water Temperature	Required pH Level	Water hardness	Required Concentration	Required Sanitizer Contact Time
Chlorine (when pH is less than or equal to 10)	Greater than or equal to 100F	Less than or equal to 10	Based on manufacturer recommendation	50 to 99 ppm	Greater than or equal to 7 seconds
Chlorine (when pH is less than or equal to 8)	Greater than or equal to 75F	Less than or equal to 8	Based on manufacturer recommendation	50 to 99 ppm	Greater than or equal to 7 seconds
Iodine	Greater than or equal to 68F	Less than or equal to 5 or based on manufacturer recommendation	Based on manufacturer recommendation	12.5 to 25 ppm	Greater than or equal to 30 seconds
Quats	Based on manufacturer recommendation	Based on manufacturer recommendation	Less than or equal to 500 ppm or based on manufacturer recommenda	Based on manufacturer recommendation	Greater than or equal to 30 seconds

			tion		

To clean and sanitize surfaces:
1. Scrape and remove food from surfaces.
2. Wash the surface with cleaning solution.
3. Rinse the surface with clean water.
4. Sanitize the item; make sure that all surfaces comes in contact with the sanitizing solution.
5. Air dry the surface.

Dishwashing Machine

Dishwashing machines sanitize by using hot water or a chemical solution. Dishwashing machines must have an easily accessible and readable data plate affixed to the machine containing operation specification information such as:
- temperature required for washing/rinsing/sanitizing
- pressure required for rinsing
- conveyor speed for conveyor machine or cycle time for stationary rack machines

Dishwashing machines must have a temperature measuring device that checks the water temperature at the manifold (where water sprays into the tank). The device must be able to indicate the temperature of both the wash and rinse tank as well as the hot water sanitizing final rinse manifold or chemical sanitizing solution tank. The temperature of the final rinse must be at least 180F. It must be at least 165F, if the dishwashing machine is a stationary-rack, single temperature machine. If the water is not hot enough, items won't be effectively sanitized; if the water is too hot, it can bake food onto the items.

Before putting items in a dishwasher, scrape food off the items (pre-soaking or rinsing the items if necessary to remove food particles). Load the dishwasher in a manner that allows all surfaces of the items to be exposed to the dishwasher's spray. Items must be air dried, towel drying can contaminate the items.

Manual Dishwashing (5 steps)

Manual dishwashing is often used to clean and sanitize large items. It must be done in a 3 compartment sink. Before washing items, you must prepare the 3 compartment sink.

Preparing a 3 Compartment Sink

1. Clean and sanitize the 3 tanks and drain boards.
2. Fill the first sink with detergent and water that is at least 110F. Follow the manufacturer's recommendation.

3. Fill the second sink with clean water if the items will be dipped instead of spray-rinsed.
4. Fill the third sink with hot water or a water and sanitizer solution.
5. Make sure there is a clock with a second hand so you can tell how long an item has been in contact with the sanitizer solution.

Cleaning and Sanitizing in a 3 Compartment Sink

1. Scrape and rinse items to remove debris or food.
2. Using a brush, cloth, or nylon scrub pad, wash the items in the first sink. Change the water and detergent as necessary (suds are gone or water appears dirty).
3. Rinse the items in the second sink. You can rinse items using a sprayer or dipping the items in the sink.
4. Sanitize items in the third sink. Never rinse items after sanitizing them; this could contaminate them.
5. Air-dry the items upside down, so water can drain. Never use a towel to dry items as that could contaminate them.

All items should be stored with their handles up. Glasses should be stored bottoms up, so staff can grab them without contaminating food contact areas. All bowls and containers must be stored upside down as well.

Cleaning Tools

Cleaning tools must be stored away from food prep areas. Mops need to be stored hanging so they can dry quickly to prevent growth of mold. There should be a utility sink for filling buckets and washing cleaning tools. There should also be a floor drain to dump dirty water. Never clean mops or other cleaning tools in sinks used for handwashing, food prep, or dishwashing. Do NOT dump mop water or other liquid waste into toilets or urinals.

Wipe Cloths

Never use cloths meant for wiping food spills for any other purpose. There are two types of wipe cloths: wet and dry. Wet cloths used to wipe counters or other equipment must be stored in a sanitizer solution between uses. Dry cloths used to wipe spills from tableware must be kept dry while in use and must not be dirty or contain food debris.

Cleaning Schedules

Create cleaning schedules so certain areas and equipment that are out of sight don't get forgotten. The schedule should state the items to be cleaned, how often items should be clean, how items should be cleaned, chemicals to use, and the person responsible for cleaning the items. Everyday, you should check that tasks listed in the cleaning schedule were completed.

Integrated Pest Management (IPM)

Work with a licensed pest control company to manage pests.

Signs of rodents: droppings, shredded paper (rodents gnaw at food packaging), etc. Rats and mice have droppings that look like black pellets and leave oily brush marks on walls and baseboards.

Signs of cockroaches: cockroaches emit an oily odor; cockroaches lay brown egg cases, their droppings look like grains of black pepper.

3 Pest Management Rules

1. Prevent pest from entering.
    a. Filling all cracks and holes.
    b. Fill gaps around pipes.
    c. Keep doors closed.
    d. All windows that will be open must have screens with 16 mesh to 1 inch.
    e. Inspect food and supply deliveries for pest; reject shipments where you found pests or signs of pests.
2. Prevent access to food and water.
    a. Clean all hard to reach places. Clean up spills immediately.
    b. Store food properly (6 inches off the ground and 6 inches away from the wall).
    c. Use FIFO to rotate products, so pests do not have time settle and breed.
    d. Keep trash cans covered and take out trash often.
    e. Do not allow water to pool, condensation from refrigerator units or air conditioning are sources of water.
3. Hire a licensed pest control company to eliminate pests found.

Facilities

Most health departments require a "plan review" to ensure all equipments meet FDA requirements and plumbing and wiring meet code. Plan reviews must be submitted for approval before construction, conversion of an existing structure, or remodeling of or change of type of food establishment. You must contact the health department before construction begins.

Floors, Walls, and Ceilings

- Floors, walls, and ceilings need to be durable and easily cleaned. Surfaces should be smooth and durable, for easier cleaning.
- Floors should be non-skid and non-porous.
- Carpeting is NOT allowed anywhere except in the dining room.

Equipment

- All food service equipment that will be in contact with food must be designed for commercial use and approved by the National Sanitation Foundation (NSF) or Underwriters Lab (UL).
- All equipment must be at least 6 inches off the floor or mounted to floor. The 6 inches allows room for you to clean under the equipment.
- All equipment on tables must be 4 inches all the table (for ease of cleaning under the equipment).

Ventilation

Ventilation is required to remove odors, smoke, gas, and moisture. Ventilation systems must be cleaned and maintained according to manufacturer instructions. Bad ventilation can cause buildup of grease and dirt on walls and ceilings.

Lighting

All lights should have shatter resistant bulbs or protective covers to prevent glass from dropping in/on food. Lighting intensity is measured in units of "foot candles" or lux.

Area	Required Light Intensity
Food prep areas	At least 50 candles
Reach-in fridge, self service areas, restrooms, utensil storage areas	At least 20 foot candles

Dry storage, refrigerated/frozen walk in storage, all areas while cleaning	At least 10 foot candles

Plumbing

Only potable (drinkable) water is allowed when preparing food or working with utensils or equipments that will come into contact with food. Water must come from an approved source, such as:

- public water system
- private water system constructed, maintained, tested according to the law
- bottled water from approved sources
- closed water containers
- commercial water transport vehicle

Cross Connections

A cross connection is the mixing of dirty and clean water. One way cross connections can occur is when a nozzle (such as those at end of spray hose) hangs down to the sink below the flood rim. If a sink is filled with water, water can be siphoned into the faucet contaminating the clean water supply. To prevent a cross connection, there should be an "air gap" between the faucet outlet and the sink flood rim. The air gap must be twice the diameter of the faucet water supply inlet or at least 1 inch, whichever is greater.

Another way to prevent cross connections is to install backflow prevention devices such as vacuum breakers, double check valves, and reduced pressure zone backflow preventers. While backflow prevention devices do help, "air gaps" are the only completely reliable way to prevent backflow. Backflow prevention devices are often installed in mop sinks and wherever an "air gap" can't be used. A trained and certified technician must check the backflow prevention devices periodically to verify that they are in working order; you must document when the backflow devices were checked.

A buildup of grease in grease traps can also cause dirty water to backflow. Grease traps should be cleaned regularly to prevent grease buildups.

Facility Plumbing Requirements

- You must have at least 1 toilet (or minimum required by jurisdiction).
- Shield overhead waste or sprinkler pipes or avoid placing them over storage and food prep areas to prevent leaks and condensation from dripping onto the area.
- At least one service sink (also called mop or utility sink) or curbed facility with a floor drain must be provided in the facility.

Garbage

- Trash cans must be covered unless in continuous use.
- Indoor trash cans must be leak-proof, waterproof, and pest-proof.
- The inside and outside of trash cans must be cleaned regularly.
- Garbage dumpsters must also be on solid foundation, such as concrete. Garbage dumpsters must be covered at all times.

Emergencies

Emergencies are imminent health hazards. Imminent health hazards are events that can cause significant health threats and require immediate correction or facility closure. Common emergencies are electrical power outages, fires, floods, and sewage backups. If you can't maintain minimum food safety, you must close immediately. Any backup of sewage is cause for immediate closure, as well as notifying the health department.

If you encounter a grease fire, cover and smother the fire; never use water to put out a grease fire.

After the emergency event:
1. Throw away spoiled or contaminated food. Throw away food where the packaging is no longer intact.
2. Bring TCS food back to the correct temperatures.
3. Clean and sanitize all contaminated equipment and surfaces. Sanitize with a bleach solution of 10:1. All cleaning tools must be sanitized after cleaning.
4. Re-establish the physical security of the building.
5. Verify that the water supply is drinkable.

Regardless of the emergency event, you must have approval from the local regulatory authorities before resuming service.

Health Policies and Practices

The Federal Drug Administration (FDA) inspects all food except meat, poultry, and eggs. The FDA is also responsible for regulating the transport of food and providing food safety regulation recommendations, called the Food Code. The US Department of Agriculture (USDA) regulates and inspects meat, poultry, and eggs. The Center for Disease Control (CDC) is responsible for developing disease prevention and control, environmental health, and health education policies. The US Public Health Service (PHS) is responsible for protecting and promoting the health and safety of the nation. The CDC and PHS investigate foodborne illness outbreaks.

Reporting Health Issues

You must tell employees, including new hires that have not started working yet, to inform management when they are ill. You may be asked to show proof that you've trained employees to report health issues. Proof can be in the form of employee signed documents where they agreed to report illness, documents showing the staff has completed training which included information about reporting illnesses, or posted signs around the food establishment reminding employees that they must report any health issues to management.

You must also have a health or illness policy that outline the actions to be taken based on the symptoms of the employee. Most health departments can provide you with a sample health or illness policy. Depending on the employee's symptoms, you may need to "restrict" or "exclude" them from working. **"Restrict"** means to limit employee activities (can't handle food, can't clean equipment/utensils, etc.). **"Exclude"** means employees can't come into work.

- If an employee has an infected cut or infected open sore, they should be restricted.
- If an employee has persistent sneezing, coughing, or runny nose, they should be restricted.
- If an employee has fever or sore throat or headache with a fever, they should be restricted. If the food establishment primarily serves high risk populations, they should be excluded.
- If an employee is experiencing diarrhea and/or vomiting, they should be excluded until they are symptom free for 24 hours or have a note from a medical provider clearing them for work.
- If an employee has jaundice, they should be excluded for at least 7 days from onset of the symptoms, unless the employee has a note from a doctor saying the jaundice is not caused by Hepatitis A. The local health department notified and the employee may return to work only after approval from the health department.
- If an employee is diagnosed with a foodborne illness caused by one of the pathogens listed below or lives with someone that has (except for nontyphoidal Salmonella), they should be excluded and the local health department should be notified. They may return to work only after approval from the health department:

- Norovirus
- Hepatitis A
- Shigella spp.
- Shiga-toxin producing E. Coli (STEC)
- Salmonella Typhi
- Nontyphoidal Salmonella

Food Recalls

Most vendors will notify you of a recall, but you should still check the FDA and USDA sites for list of food recalls. When you are notified of a food recall, remove the item and store it in an area separate from food, utensils, equipments, and single-use items. Place a "Do Not Use" and "Do Not Discard" label on the items to prevent it from being used. Follow the manufacturer instructions on what to do with the product.

Foodborne Illness Outbreaks

If you receive more than 1 foodborne illness complaint, you may have an outbreak. If a foodborne illness outbreak occurs, you must do the following:
1. Gather the following information from the person making the complaint: contact information, food or drink that was eaten, date that the person first became sick, and the symptoms experienced.
2. Notify authorities.
3. Place a "Do Not Use" and "Do Not Discard" label on the suspected food product.
4. Document the following information about the suspected product: product description, production date, lot number, pack size, and sell-by date.
5. Identify a list of food handlers working at the time of the suspected contamination. They should be interviewed immediately by management about their health status. They will also likely be interviewed by investigators.
6. Review food handling procedures to determine where things may have gone wrong.

HACCP - Hazard Analysis Critical Control Point

HACCP is a 7 step food hazard prevention system. The 7 steps are:
1. Hazard Analysis: identify hazards biological, chemical, physical that are likely to cause illness
2. Critical Control Points: identify CCPs that are necessary to prevent or eliminate the hazard. CCPs are points in the food handling process where the loss of control may result in health risks. CCPs are control measures such as cooking/cooling, time and temperature controls, etc.
3. Critical Limits: a numeric value (min or max) that is required to prevent or reduce hazard (e.g. required cooking temperatures).

4. Establish Procedures: act of observing or making measurements to determine if critical limits are met.
5. Establish Corrective Actions: actions that must be taken if critical limits are not met.
6. Verify the system works.
7. Develop a record keeping system.

Practice Test

1.You are cooking ground beef for immediate service. What are the temperature requirements?

A. There is no temperature requirement.
B. 145F for 15 seconds
C. 155F for 15 seconds
D. 165F for 15 seconds

2. How often should you check the temperature of PHF held in a buffet or self service area?

A. every 2 hours
B. every 4 hours
C. every 6 hours
D. every 8 hours

3. One of your worker has the flu, should you report this to the authorities?
A. yes
B. no

4. Only food with a temperature below 75F can be stored in a refrigerator?
A. true
B. false

5. Glasses/cups should be stored upside down and utensils should be stored with handles up.
A. true
B. false

6. You are required to notify authorities if you get more than how many foodborne illness complaints?
A. 1
B. 2
C. 5
D. 10

7. Unpasteurized juice may be served to high risk populations as long as you provide a consumer advisory.
A. True
B. False

8. Using hair spray away from food and food prep areas is one way of preventing what?
A. biological contamination
B. physical contamination
C. chemical contamination
D. cross contamination

9. You are frying pork for immediate service. What are the temperature requirements?
A. There is no temperature requirement.
B. 145F for 15 seconds
C. 155F for 15 seconds
D. 165F for 15 seconds

10. What must the interior temperature of a refrigerator be?
A. between 36F and 37F in the coolest part of the unit
B. between 36F and 37F in the warmest part of the unit
C. between 38F and 39F in the coolest part of the unit
D. between 38F and 39F in the warmest part of the unit

11. What is the maximum time bread can be kept in the temperature danger zone?
A. there is no maximum time
B. 2 hours
C. 4 hours
D. 8 hours

12. Which of the following are ways to prevent toxin poisoning? Choose all that apply.
A. freeze food
B. cook food thoroughly
C. buy from reputable vendors
D. make sure employees practice proper hygiene

13. How hot should water be when washing your hands?
A. 100F or greater
B. 130F or greater
C. 135F or greater
D. 140F or greater

14. Pasta cooked for hot holding should reach what temperature?
A. 135F
B. 145F
C. 155F
D. 165F

15. Which of the following is NOT a source of food/water for pests?
A. cardboard boxes
B. condensation from air conditioning units
C. residue on equipment
D. dirty wet mop

16. What food safety subjects should employees be trained on? Choose all that apply.
A. Proper hand washing
B. Proper hygiene
C. Cleaning and Sanitizing
D. Food Time/Temperature Control
E. Cross contamination prevention
F. Food Handling Practices

17. What is a measure of light intensity?
A. a watt
B. a joule
C. a light candle
D. a foot candle

18. Meat and poultry must have the USDA inspection stamp.
A. True
B. False

19. There is an uncontained sewage backup at your food establishment. What should be done?
A. notify authorities and wait for them to tell you what actions to take
B. immediately close and notify authorities
C. continue operating if sewage backup is not near food or food prep area
D. clean up sewage and continue operating

20. From top to bottom, how should food be stored in a refrigerator?
A. whole chicken, ground meat, whole cuts of beef/pork, whole fish, RTE food
B. RTE food, whole cuts of beef/pork, whole fish, ground meat, whole chicken
C. RTE food, whole fish, whole cuts of beef/pork, ground meat, whole chicken
D. RTE food, whole fish, whole cuts of beef/pork, whole chicken, ground meat

21. What is a cross connection?
A. mixing of raw meat and ready to eat food
B. where 2 pipes meet
C. where hot and cold water pipes converge
D. mixing of potable and waste water

22. When using the heat method (using plain water) to sanitize items in a ware-washing machine, what temperature should the water be?
A. 171F
B. Between 180F and 194F
C. Between 75F and 120F
D. Greater than 75F

23. You are cooking whole chicken for immediate service. What are the temperature requirements?
A. There is no temperature requirement.
B. 145F for 15 seconds
C. 155F for 15 seconds
D. 165F for 15 seconds

24. How many hours do you have to cool cooked PHFs?
A. 2 hours
B. 4 hours
C. 6 hours to cool from above 135F to below 41F
D. 2 hours to cool from above 135F to 70F, then 4 hours to cool from 70F to below 41F

25. What are the cooking requirements for unpasteurized eggs? Choose all that apply.
A. unpasteurized eggs prepped for immediate service need to reach a temperature of 145F for 15 seconds
B. unpasteurized shell eggs that will be placed in hot holding need to reach a temperature of 155F for 15 seconds
C. unpasteurized eggs prepped for immediate service need to reach a temperature of 135F for 15 seconds
D. unpasteurized shell eggs that will be placed in hot holding need to reach a temperature of 145F for 15 seconds

26. A tuna salad was prepared on May 2 using tuna that was prepared on May 1, what should the discard date be?
A. May 7
B. May 8
C. May 9
D. May 10

27. When not in use, food contact surfaces should be?
A. covered and free of physical contaminants
B. cleaned every 4 hours
C. sanitized every 4 hours
D. cleaned and sanitized every 4 hours

28. One day after eating undercooked chicken, Jason has a fever and diarrhea. What is Jason most likely suffering from?
A. allergic reaction
B. foodborne infection
C. foodborne intoxication
D. chemical contamination

29. Viruses do not require a host to multiply.
a. True
b. False

30. Which of these is more likely to be found in poultry?
A. e. coli
B. trichinella
C. salmonella
D. ciguatera

31. A customer finds a cockroach in his/her pasta. What is this an example of?
A. biological contamination
B. chemical contamination
C. physical contamination
D. cross contamination

32. Which of the following are signs of rodents? Choose all that apply.
A. shredded paper near food packaging
B. black pellet like droppings
C. oily odor
D. oily brush marks on walls and baseboards

33. During transportation, ground beef was held at a temperature of 80F for 2 hours. After receiving the ground beef package, how long do you have to inspect the package and store the ground beef or prepare it for cooking, before the ground beef needs to be discarded?
A. 2 hours
B. 4 hours
C. 6 hours
D. 8 hours

34. Which of these are examples of PHF?
A. sliced tomatoes
B. garlic in oil
C. steak
D. baked potatoes

35. Which of the following are proper ways to thaw food? Choose all that apply.
A. thaw in refrigerator, maintaining a temperature of 41F or lower
B. submerge food in a bucket of cold water; water must cover at least half of food
C. thaw food in microwave as long as food will be immediately cooked
D. thaw food as part of cooking process

36. A food handler must wash their hands after:
A. Serving customers
B. Clearing tables
C. After putting on single use gloves
D. None of the above.

37. Which one of these employees should you exclude from work?
A. An employee, without a fever, who has persistent sneezing, coughing, and runny nose.
B. An employee who is experiencing vomiting or diarrhea.
C. An employee with infected open sore.
D. All of the above.

38. Cooked chicken can be held without temperature control if:
A. Cooked chicken can never be held without temperature control.
B. It is served or thrown out within 6 hours.
C. It is served or thrown out within 4 hours.

39. What is the best way to prevent backflow? Select only one.
A. Install a backflow prevention device.
B. Create a cross connection.
C. Create an air gap.
D. None of the above.

40. Food cooked during the initial cooking stage of partial cooking, should not be cooked for longer than?
A. 45 minutes
B. 60 minutes
C. 120 minutes
D. None of the above

Answers and Explanations

1. C. There are no temperature requirements when reheating food for immediate service. However, there are temperature requirements for cooking food, even for immediate service. Whole or ground chicken needs to be cooked to 165F for 15 seconds. Any other ground meat must be cooked to 155F for 15 seconds. Any other meat must be cooked to 145F for 15 seconds.

2. B. You should check the temperature of PHFs in hot or cold holding every 4 hours. Hot food must be held at temperature of 135F or higher. Ff hot food drops below 135F for more than 4 hours, it must be discarded; if less than 4 hours, it can be reheated. Cold food must be held at a temperature of 41F or lower. If cold food stays below 41F, it may be held for 7 days.

3. B. The flu is not a reportable illness. The reportable illnesses are salmonella, e.coli, shigella, hepatitis A, norovirus

4. B. Food must have a temperature below 70F before being stored in a refrigerator. Otherwise, you risk raising the temperature of the refrigerator.

5. A. Glasses/cups should be stored upside down and utensils should be stored with handles up. This allows people to grab items without contaminating food contact surfaces.

6. A. You are required to notify authorities if you get more than 1 foodborne illness complaint.

7. B. Unpasteurized juice may NOT be served to high risk populations; even if a consumer advisory is provided. Unpasteurized juice may be served to the general population if a consumer advisory is provided.

8. C. Ways to prevent chemical contamination include using hair spray, lotions, cleaners, etc. away from food or food prep areas; following manufacturer directions/safety precautions for all chemicals; not storing acidic food in metal containers such as copper, brass, tin, galvanized cookware.

9. B. There are no temperature requirements when reheating food for immediate service. However, there are temperature requirements for cooking food, even for immediate service. Whole or ground chicken needs to be cooked to 165F for 15 seconds. Any other ground meat must be cooked to 155F for 15 seconds. Any other meat must be cooked to 145F for 15 seconds.

10. D. The interior of a refrigerator must be between 38F and 39F in the warmest part of the unit.

11. A. Bread is not considered a potentially hazardous food and does not have a maximum allowable time it can spend in the temperature danger zone. PHFs can spend a maximum of 4 hours in the temperature danger zone (6 hours if food remains below 70F). The 4 hours include time it took to receive/inspect food, prepare food, etc. The 4-hour clock starts over once food is brought to temperature outside of danger zone.

12. C. Toxins cannot be killed by freezing nor heat. Toxins are usually not caused/transferred due to bad hygiene.

13. A. You should wash your hands for 20 seconds (10-15 seconds of rubbing) using hot water at a temperature of 100F or greater; 120F or greater in CA

14. A. Fruits/vegetables/grains/pasta intended for hot holding should be cooked to 135F.

15. A. Dirty wet mops, residue on equipments, condensation from air conditioning units are all sources of water and/or food for pests.

16. A,B,C,D,E,F. Employees should be trained in all of the following subjects: proper hand washing, proper hygiene, cleaning/sanitizing, food time/temperature control, cross contamination prevention, food handling practices.

17. D. A foot candle is a measure of light intensity

18. A. True. All meat/poultry must meet USDA inspection requirements.

19. B. A sewage backup is immediate cause for closure and notifying authorities. Any time, you can't maintain minimum food safety, you must close immediately.

20. C. Store food according to how high cooking temperature needs to be (RTE at top, whole fish, whole cuts of beef/pork, ground meat/fish, whole or ground chicken at bottom).

21. What is a cross connection?
Answer: D. mixing of potable and waste water
Explanation: Cross connection is the mixing of clean and dirty water.

22. B. When using the heat method (using plain water) to sanitize items in a dishwashing machine, the water should be between 180F and 194F. When using the heat method in a 3 bay sink, items must be submerged in hot water (171F) for at least 30 seconds

23. D. There are no temperature requirements when reheating food for immediate service. However, there are temperature requirements for cooking food, even for immediate service. Whole or ground chicken needs to be cooked to 165F for 15 seconds. Any other ground meat must be cooked to 155F for 15 seconds. Any other meat must be cooked to 145F for 15 seconds.

24. D. PHFs must be cooled from above 135F to 70F within 2 hours, and then cooled from 70F to below 41F within 4 hours. If you don't cool food within the time limit, the food must be discarded or re-heated (following correct re-heating procedures).

25. A, B. Unpasteurized eggs prepared for immediate service need to reach a temperature of 145F for 15 seconds. Unpasteurized shell eggs that will be placed in hot holding need to reach a temperature of 155F for 15 seconds

26. A. The discard date should be May 7. Salads and ready to eat food that contain PHF should be discarded 7 days(inclusive) from when original PHF (i.e.chicken/tuna) was cooked/cooled, not date salad was assembled.

27. A. When not in use, food contact surfaces should be covered. When food contact surfaces are in continual use, they should be cleaned and sanitized every 4 hours.

28. B. Foodborne infections are caused by eating food that contains living pathogens and symptoms have a delayed onset (they do not occur right away). Foodborne intoxication is caused by eating food that contain toxins; symptoms usually occur rapidly. Allergic reactions usually occur within minutes to hours after eating food a person is allergic to.

29. B. Viruses do NOT require a host to live, but DO require a host to multiply.

30. C. Salmonella is likely to be found in poultry/eggs. E. coli is more likely found in beef and produce. Trichinella is more likely found in pork and wild game. Ciguateria poisoning is more likely to occur when eating fish.

31. C. Any contaminant that can be seen is considered a physical contamination.

32. A,B,D. Oily odor is not a sign of rodents; it is a sign of cockroaches

33. A. Ground beef is a potentially hazardous food. Since the ground beef spent 2 hours in the temperature danger zone during delivery, you have 2 hours to bring the ground beef outside the temperature danger zone before it must be discarded. PHFs can spend a maximum of 4 hours in the temperature danger zone (6 hours if food remains below 70F). The 4 hours include time it took to receive/inspect food, prepare food, etc. The 4-hour clock starts over once food is brought to a temperature outside of danger zone.

34. A,B,C,D. PHF tend to be high in protein, includes heat treated plant foods (cooked vegetables/fruits such as baked potatoes, baked beans), include cut melons/fruit, raw sprouts (alfalfa, bean, radish), tofu, soy burgers, cut leafy greens, garlic in oil(potential for botulism)

35. A,C,D. The 4 ways to thaw food are:
1. in refrigerator (maintaining temp of 41F or lower)
2. completely submerged under cold RUNNING water (water must be below 70F)
3. in microwave as long as food goes immediately into cooking process
4. as part of cooking process

36. B. A food handler must wash their hands after handling dirty items. Clearing tables usually requires you to handle dirty items. Serving customers does not necessarily mean you will come in contact with dirty items.

37. B. An employee who is experiencing vomiting or diarrhea should be excluded from work until they are symptom free for 24 hours or have a doctor's note. Employees with infected open sores or have persistent sneezing, coughing, or runny nose should be restricted.

38. C. Hot food can be served without temperature control if it is served or thrown out within 4 hours. Cold food can be served without temperature control if it is served or thrown out within 6 hours.

39. C. While backflow prevention devices do help prevent backflow, air gaps are the only completely reliable way to prevent backflow.

40. B. Food should not be cooked longer than 60 minutes in the initial cooking stage of partial cooking.

Thank You For Your Purchase

Thank you for your purchase. If you found this study guide helpful, please leave a review for us on Amazon; we would truly appreciate it.

If you have any questions or concerns, please contact us at goldstartestprep@gmail.com.

Bibliography

Berger, Lisa M. and Cynthia Parenteau. Food Safety For Managers. Boston, 2017.

Kivett, Joe and Mark Tamplin. The Food Safety Book: What You Don't Know Could Kill You. 2016.

National Restaurant Association. Servsafe Manager 7th Edition. Chicago, 2017.

Premier Food Safety, 2017. http://www.premierfoodsafety.com.

Made in the USA
Middletown, DE
15 October 2021